The fight against drugs is of more fundamental importance today than ever before. Drugs are a source of pain, suffering and social isolation for too many people, especially the young. Though we cannot dispense with punitive measures, we must try to understand the underlying social malaise and the reasons behind this scourge if we are to develop a comprehensive strategy to combat it.

The European Union is committed to doing just that. Though it cannot hope to solve the problem on its own, it can, through active cooperation, give considerable help to the Member States, local and regional authorities and society at large in their fight against drug trafficking and abuse.

In accordance with the principle of subsidiarity, the measures taken by the European Union focus on:

- trade relations,

- cooperation with other countries, international organizations and non-governmental organizations, and

- prevention, training and cooperation with individuals and organizations working with people affected by this problem.

The Union also has a special role to play as a provider of information. By helping to raise awareness, supplying information directly to the public and giving them the opportunity to become actively involved in the fight against drugs, the Union can help ensure that whatever measures are taken have an effective and positive outcome.

The purpose of this brochure is to show what initiatives the European Union has taken in this field. I hope it will stimulate people, particularly those in civil society, to think about the issues and help us to do more and do it better.

We decided to publish the brochure as part of 'Building Europe together', one of the priority information campaigns. After all, building Europe is not just about institutions, procedures and markets. It is, above all, a joint venture to create a society based on the very diversity from which we derive our strength and our great ability to tackle social problems, and on the values shared by all Europeans.

Marcelino Oreja,
Member of the European Commission

A great deal of additional information on the European Union is available on the Internet. It can be accessed through the Europa server (http://europa.eu.int).

Cataloguing data can be found at the end of this publication.

Luxembourg: Office for Official Publications of the European Communities, 1997

ISBN 92-828-0426-7

Printed in Germany

PRINTED ON WHITE CHLORINE-FREE PAPER

CONTENTS

Fears among European Union citizens

EUR 15

Fear	Percentage
Increase in drugs/organized crime	69%
More taxes	68%
Loss of small farms	62%
Loss of small/medium-sized businesses	57%
Loss of fisheries	57%
Deeper economic crisis	56%
Slower decisions due to increased bureaucracy	56%
Loss of social benefits	56%
Decisions imposed by larger Member States	56%
Transfer of jobs to low cost member countries	55%
Expansion to the east costing too much	52%
Transfer of jobs to low cost non-member countries	52%
Cheaper but lower quality imports	50%
More foreign workers	47%
People too different to get along	45%
End of national currency	44%
Richer Member States paying for others	43%
Too much central control	42%
Loss of power for smaller Member States	41%
Massive imports from other member countries	40%
Massive imports from non-member countries	38%
Loss of national identity and culture	35%
Too rapid change	35%
Own language used less	33%
Removal of border controls	33%
Other countries joining EU	30%
Own country not existing any more	30%

Source: Survey No 44 Mega-Fieldwork January-March 1996,
Eurobarometer 45, 1996

Introduction

An active approach, in response to European citizens' concerns

This booklet describes the anti-drugs action of the European Union (EU) in terms of the concerns of citizens. It addresses these themes:

› what does the citizen want in relation to **action on drug users**?

› what does the citizen want in relation to **action against drug trafficking**?

› what does the citizen want as far as **international action** on drugs is concerned?

› and, finally, what **information** does the European citizen want in order to contribute to drug policy debates? And what information is wanted by policy-makers who serve the citizen in order to maximize the coordination, impact and effectiveness of drug policies in Europe?

Action by the EU addresses each of these issues of concern. The EU has done much in the past, and is doing more today. The EU is spending more money on health-related aspects of drug problems; the EU is doing more to promote cooperation in criminal justice against drug trafficking; the EU is promoting more programmes and assistance in international policies; and, finally, the EU is doing more in the way of information exchange on drugs.

This booklet explains the main strands of these actions on drugs. Such actions have developed over the years, following the lead given by the European Council, the European Parliament and the European Commission, developments in EU Member States and activities of the international partners of the EU. Additionally, the European Monitoring Centre for Drugs and Drug Addiction (EMCDDA) facilitates information exchange on the drug trends, practical responses to drug users, and national strategies and policies.

Together with the Member States, their regional and local authorities, non-governmental organizations and specialist centres, European Union institutions and bodies have developed a comprehensive approach to drug strategies and policies, reflecting the concerns of European citizens.

A coordinated approach, to maximize cooperation and value

By the late 1980s, the involvement of the European Community in action against drugs was developing fast, along the lines to be described within this booklet. Member States were also taking urgent action, at the level of local communities, regional administrations, national authorities and international cooperation. This raised the question of the coherence and coordination of all this activity.

In 1989 the late French President Mitterrand sent a letter to all the other European Community Heads of State, calling for a coordinated strategy. He drew attention to some important tasks: getting agreement on how to define 'addiction' and how to respond to it; the need for each Member State to set up a national drugs coordination office; agreement on a Community policy against money laundering; tighter controls at the external borders of the Community; and acceleration of the implementation of international conventions.

Political agreement came quickly, and by the end of 1990, the 'first **European action plan to combat drugs**' had been adopted by the Community. This action plan has been updated twice, the most recent version being agreed by Heads of State in 1995.

The action plan is founded on four components:

> demand reduction (meaning preventive and other action in relation to drug use);

> supply reduction (through the targeting of trafficking networks and related problems);

> international action on the world stage;

> and the pooling and sharing of information and knowledge amongst policy-makers, professionals and citizens of the European Union.

Because it is a straightforward and authoritative framework for presentation of EU action on drugs, the current action plan 1995-99 has been adopted as the framework for this booklet.

More recently, in 1992, the Treaty on European Union (Maastricht Treaty) put action against drugs into an EU Treaty for the first time. This puts such action at the heart of the European Union's political commitments, as well as consolidating existing policies, especially in relation to public health and cross-border drug trafficking.

Finally, in June 1997, the draft Treaty of Amsterdam sought to strengthen these provisions. These changes will in future be reflected in a revised version of the action plan. Meanwhile, this booklet gives European citizens a broad overview of EU action against drugs within the EU and in the broader international context.

10 years of action

1987 ›
The European Economic Community (EEC) is a participant in the Vienna Conference on the illicit trade in narcotic drugs and psychotropic substances.

The EEC makes its first financial contribution to the international fight against drugs.

1988 ›
The EEC is a signatory to the United Nations Convention against the illicit trade in narcotic drugs and psychotropic substances (Article 12).

At the initiative of the European Parliament, a specific line to combat drugs is created in the European budget.

1989 ›
The European Committee to Combat Drugs (ECCD) is set up, bringing together the national coordinators from the EEC Member States.

1990 ›
Measures are taken by the Community to prevent the diversion of certain chemicals for the illicit manufacture of narcotic drugs and psychotropic substances. (Regulation EEC/3677/90)

The European Council adopts the first European plan to combat drugs during its Rome session.

1991 ›
Directive 91/308/EEC, aimed at preventing the financial system from being used for money laundering, comes into force.

1992 ›
The Treaty on European Union, which refers to the fight against drug addiction, is signed in Maastricht.

The Directive on the manufacture and marketing of certain substances used in the illicit manufacture of narcotic drugs and psychotropic substances comes into force (92/109/EEC).

1993 ›
The European Monitoring Centre for Drugs and Drug Addiction (EMCDDA) is set up.

1994 ›
A new global European Union action plan to combat drugs (1995-1999).

1995 ›
The European Council, meeting in Madrid, gives a fresh impetus to the European Union's fight against drugs.

A conference on the policies on drugs is organized jointly by the European Parliament, the Presidency of the EU Council of Ministers and the European Commission.

1996 ›
Europol Convention is ratified and several agreements are struck on better coordination of police and customs services. New funding agreed for drug action in health and criminal justice contexts. More international action.

The fight against drugs is one of the top priorities of the EU's Irish Presidency.

First programme of Community action on the prevention of drug dependence adopted in December

1997 ›
Amsterdam meeting of Heads of State agrees new draft Treaty containing improvement to actions on drugs.

The Council adopts a common action to exchange rapid information and to control new synthetic drugs.

1

Reducing drug use and reducing health risks

Citizens of the European Union justifiably expect the Union to take appropriate action in order to safeguard public health.

In the light of recent public health scares, people want a high level of health protection. European Community action will be directed towards improving public health, preventing illness or diseases and obviating sources of danger to human health. Furthermore, the Community shall complement the Member States' action in reducing drug-related damage through information and prevention.

These terms can summarize the way in which European citizens' expectations were understood by the EU during the summer of 1997, as representatives of the Member States reached agreement on the draft of a new Treaty, which will provide the framework for action on drugs in future years.

In fact, the involvement of the European Community in public health matters concerning drugs goes back many years. With growing public concern over drugs, political leaders responded by including a specific clause on the prevention of drug dependence in the 1992 Maastricht Treaty. Prevention can mean any activity which reduces the demand for drugs, for example school-based drug education, or public information.

In 1997 the draft Treaty of Amsterdam reiterated and widened the focus of concern, with a specific mention of 'reducing drug-related damage'. This reference to what is sometimes called 'harm reduction' or 'risk reduction' is a response, in particular, to the serious health risks posed by communicable diseases such as AIDS.

Adopting this perspective, we can say that:

› European citizens want a reduction in the health risks that face drug users and the wider society (such as the transmission of infectious diseases through the sharing of non-sterile injection equipment);

› they want a reduction in drug use itself (especially heavier drug use, drug dependence, and related social, occupational, financial and family problems);

› and they want a reduction in the demand for illegal drugs (since drug users searching for drugs to consume stimulate more supply).

The following paragraphs focus on health-related aspects of EU policies. Later in this booklet there is an outline of cooperation on enforcement measures against supply and on international aspects.

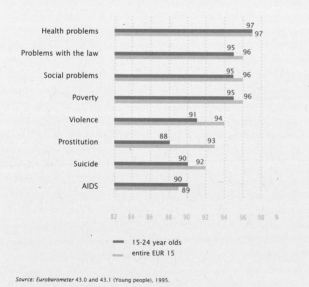

Citizens' beliefs about drug use

'the consumption of drugs can lead to:'

Health problems	97 / 97
Problems with the law	95 / 96
Social problems	95 / 96
Poverty	95 / 96
Violence	91 / 94
Prostitution	88 / 93
Suicide	90 / 92
AIDS	90 / 89

82 84 86 88 90 92 94 96 98 %

— 15-24 year olds
▬ entire EUR 15

Source: Eurobarometer 43.0 and 43.1 (Young people), 1995.

1.1. Action so far in relation to drug users

From the early years since its formation in the 1950s, the European Community gave some support to programmes of assistance to drug users, within the context of training and rehabilitation for re-entry into employment.

For example, funds were channelled to rehabilitation agencies in the Member States through the Social Fund, which supports programmes of training for employment for economically and socially marginalized people — those who have never had employment or who have at some stage fallen out of employment. Heavy users and dependent users of drugs such as heroin quite often find themselves in this situation. Non-governmental agencies, charities, foundations and other voluntary groups have received financial support from the European Community, in order to run programmes of social rehabilitation and employment training for drug users.

> **Action on drugs in the context of free movement of people**

Drug users do not always stay in their country of origin. Nationals of one Member State may move to another, for reasons that may include a search for work, and/or a search for social and health services. Some of these mobile drug users are also involved in drug trafficking, in a small or a big way. This can pose a challenge to the regions and cities in which they settle: not only because of the financial costs that may be implied in providing health and other services, but also because of the possibility of an impact on public order.

So, during the 1970s, some national authorities began to ask if they could deport nationals of another Member State, on the grounds that they have been involved in drug trafficking. On this question, the Court of Justice of the European Communities heard several cases involving drugs.

Typically, cases entailed a person facing a deportation order, following a criminal conviction for an offence involving the possession of illegal drugs or, more seriously, trafficking in drugs. In all these cases, the Court found that deportations could only be justified if the conduct of the person concerned posed an imminent and serious threat to public order, public security or public health. In such cases, a Member State national's right to move freely within the European Community, for example as a worker or someone seeking employment, was primary.

The mobility of drug users points to the need to provide health services for them, to try to improve their general health (both for their own good, and that of the wider community), and to reduce their drug use and any involvement they have in trafficking. In the last few years, the situation has, if anything, become more pressing.

> **Action in relation to 'drug tourism'**

By the 1990s, the drug phenomenon had expanded in size and scope in all the Member States. And, with increasing free movement of people, following the single market in 1992, the phenomenon that became known as 'drug tourism' became problematic in some parts of the EU — particularly in some border regions and cities.

Not only does this present challenges to criminal justice systems, but it can also lead to public nuisance and public health problems, due to the congregation of drug users in one area. Inevitably, some drug users, particularly injectors, have a heightened risk of having health problems; some are infectious or carry contagious diseases; and some drop injection equipment after using it, which can be highly dangerous if picked up by children, in particular. Of course, these problems can also accompany drug users who stay in their localities or towns of origin, or who are mobile within their Member State. But, from the point of view of the public, 'outsiders' may be more socially visible than local people who use drugs. Discriminatory feelings may be evoked, which are mapped onto underlying problems of public health and public order, and which complicate the task of policy-making.

In such cases, the EU, Member States and local administrations try to balance:

› on the one hand, the rights of the persons who use drugs, and the need for them to have access to health services;

› and, on the other hand, the rights of the wider community and its need for health protection and social tranquillity.

To find this balance is not easy, and opinions differ as to exactly where the balance should be:

› some favour the greatest degree of open access by drug users to helping and health services, even if this may result in greater inconvenience to other citizens (who will need a high degree of understanding of the situation, if they are to tolerate it);

› in other cities, regions or Member States, where there may be a stronger feeling against drug users, policy-makers are more prepared to move fast against even quite small congregations of drug users — even if this has the effect of scaring some users away from health services which might otherwise have assisted them;

› today, in many Member States, a mixed strategy is attempted. Compromises are explored, in which policy-makers try to integrate drug users into helping services and into mainstream society, in ways that minimize the affront and danger to other citizens.

In general, it has become more common for national, regional and municipal administrations to cooperate to reduce and ultimately prevent the mobility of heavy and dependent drug users (some of whom are also drug traders in a small way, or even traffickers in substantial quantities).

Such cooperation exists today between the public health authorities and other parts of the administration in several parts of the EU, for example between northern Italy and the bordering countries, between Germany and its eastern neighbours, and within the Benelux area.

This cooperation is similar in kind to well-established forms of cooperation within Member States, when cities and regions work together to reduce the load experienced by particular areas, to which heavy, 'mobile' drug users may be attracted.

In all cases, local, regional and national policy-makers want to avoid unnecessary mistakes. This makes it more important for them to learn as much as possible from other European cities and regions. Who has tried what, and with what effects? This provides a big opportunity for the EU to add value, by facilitating contacts, flows of knowledge, and the pooling of experience. Networks of health professionals, networks of city-level correspondents on municipal drug problems, and networks for research have been supported over the years.

› Action on public health

At the end of 1996, the **Community action programme on prevention of drug dependence 1996-2000** was agreed. Public health is at the core of the programme, which is to be funded over the five-year period with ECU 27 million. The programme's overall objective is to encourage cooperation between organizations from different Member States concerned with drug prevention and health, and to promote coordination between the Member States in this field. It is also open to countries of Central and Eastern Europe having applied for EU membership. It sets out two fields of work: data, research and evaluation; information, health education and training.

On 'data, research and evaluation', the programme's aim is to improve knowledge of the phenomenon of drugs and drug dependence, its consequences and methods of prevention. The programme identifies a need to share information and experience among the various groups involved in the prevention of drug dependence. This means professionals working in the helping professions, and also all other people who interact with drug users or who provide preventive drug education. Families and guardians, for instance, are singled out as people who can have 'a long-term positive influence'.

Number of drug-related deaths and population at risk

Country	pop. (million)	Number of deaths									
		1985	1986	1987	1988	1989	1990	1991	1992	1993	1994
Austria	7.9	—	—	—	—	20	36	70	121	130	140
Belgium	10.1	12	20	17	37	49	96	85	75	76	46
Denmark	5.2	150	109	140	135	123	115	188	208	210	264
Finland	5.1	4	14	15	12	24	38	62	57	50	66
France	59.3	172	185	228	236	318	350	411	499	454	564
Germany	81.1	324	348	442	670	991	1 491	2 125	2 099	1 738	1 624
Greece	10.4	10	28	56	62	72	66	79	79	78	146
Ireland	3.5	–	–	–	–	–	44	44	53	42	–
Italy	57.1	242	292	543	809	974	1 161	1 383	1 217	888	840
Luxembourg	0.4	1	3	5	4	8	9	17	17	14	29
Netherlands	15.4	28	39	16	25	27	32	41	36	31	37
Portugal	9.8	–	18	22	33	52	82	143	155	100	142
Spain	39.1	143	163	234	337	455	455	579	556	442	388
Sweden	8.7	150	138	141	125	113	143	147	175	181	205
United Kingdom	58.0	—	—	—	1 212	1 189	1 280	1 369	1 421	–	–

Due to differences in methodology these figures cannot be directly compared. For some countries they may be underestimates.
In most cases only overdoses or poisonings due to illegal drugs are included.

– = data not available
— = data available but not comparable with other years

Source: Annual Report on the state of the drugs problem in the European Union — 1995, EMCDDA, 1996.

The programme aims to support action to:

› identify factors associated with heavy and habitual drug use;

› reduce the risks associated with the injection of drugs;

› prevent damage to the foetus and prevent the transmission of infections to the unborn child of drug-using women;

› evaluate methods and programmes for prevention and risk reduction in the management of drug-dependent prisoners;

› assess health sector interventions, in particular substitution programmes (a form of treatment under which addicts are prescribed a pharmaceutical alternative to their drug of addiction).

The social, mental and physical rehabilitation and reintegration of ex-drug users back into society are also highlighted as areas where exchanges of experience and evaluation must be undertaken. Ex-addicts are vulnerable to falling back into old habits of drug use, and the programme identified this as an area where research could help to find solutions.

On 'information, health education and training', the prevention programme's aim is to contribute to improving information, education and training aimed at preventing drug dependence and its associated risks. One of the programme's avenues for the provision of drug-related information will be the European Drug Prevention Week, due to be staged again in Autumn 1998. The programme will also be giving support to teacher training in relation to drug education, and it has identified certain groups on which to focus, including young people and particularly vulnerable groups. Certain approaches to provision of information, such as street-level activities, which have been shown to be more readily utilized by socially marginal or excluded groups, will be supported (telephone helplines, etc.).

Alongside the prevention programme, the European Community is also running several other programmes that bear upon drug problems in the sphere of public health. For example, a programme on health promotion, with an ECU 35 million budget, includes action on drugs as one element. There is also a five-year work programme on the prevention of AIDS and other communicable diseases. This is partially concerned with drug injection and support projects, such as the carrying out of an analysis of risk factors among female drug injectors, and the training of social workers in counselling drug users with HIV/AIDS.

›   **Broader research programmes**

Some broader trends in drug research in the EU can be briefly mentioned, drawing on a recent review conducted for the European Commission and the European Monitoring Centre for Drugs and Drug Addiction under the aegis of the European University Institute. In many EU Member States, the trends have been the following:

›   First, from the 1970s onwards, drugs are perceived as a quite new phenomenon. The emphasis is on measuring the extent of, nature of and trends in drug use. This involves quantitative research and qualitative studies of drug users, and research on people in treatment.

›   As time goes on, the problem is seen in a broader light, social as well as medical. Research on drug prevention, social and cultural processes, drug markets and law enforcement come to the fore. This seemed to be the situation in at least some of the Member States in the 1980s or 1990s.

›   In a third possible phase, which in many Member States has not yet been reached, the evaluation of the effectiveness of control strategies is perceived as a research requirement. So is research on their costs and hence their cost-effectiveness. Also, researchers attempt integration of different perspectives, in order to give an overall view of problems and responses.

Also, as European action against drugs grows, comparative and cross-national research questions become more important. This raises the question of the basis of European research coordination and funding. Several suggestions have been made, including: identifying some priority drug research requirements by consulting the research ministries of Member States (which is an important approach at the present time); trying to identify all the drug research possibilities in all parts of the EU's broader research programmes (the fifth framework programme); or identifying research questions in each of the EU's areas of policy and action. At Community level, certain aspects of biomedical and drug detection research, epidemiological research (into drug use and drug users) and sociological research have been identified as worth supporting. But a lot of other research remains steered by the particular concerns of Member States' ministries and other authorities, by the political concerns of the moment, by the willingness of foundations to fund research, and by the interests of individual researchers.

1.2. Recent developments in public health

›   **The draft Treaty of Amsterdam**

The draft Treaty reaffirms that health protection has to be taken into account in the implementation of all other Community policies. It also says that a high level of human health protection shall be ensured in the definition and implementation of all Community policies and activities. Specifically in relation to drugs, the draft Treaty says that the European Community shall complement Member States' actions in reducing drug-related health damage, including information and prevention.

So, for the first time, reduction of drug-related damage is explicitly mentioned in a treaty. It is too early at the time of writing this booklet to say in detail what this might mean for drugs (bearing in mind that the Treaty as a whole is due to take effect in 1999). However, it can at least be said that 'risk reduction' and 'harm reduction' measures — measures adopted in order to reduce communicable diseases and other health problems associated with drug use — are now sufficiently acceptable to find expression in a treaty. All this means that, whilst the main emphasis remains the prevention of drug use (and drug supply), the EU also sees harm reduction as an objective for cooperation. This increases the protection given to every citizen; not only those who use drugs, but all of us.

2

Cooperation to reduce drug supply within the EU

Drug trafficking is one of many major problems that confront the Union. EU citizens are concerned about crime, organized or small scale, and they expect the Union to take action on this front.

People want to live in a Union in which their fundamental rights are fully respected. They also want to live and move freely within the Union, without fear of threats to their personal safety. Racism and xenophobia, as well as crime and criminal activities, such as terrorism, offences against children, drug trafficking and fraud, transcend national borders within the Union. The Union must therefore be able to extend as necessary across those borders the protection of its citizens against such scourges, and provide them with a high level of safety.

Responding to these concerns, the draft Treaty foresees: improvements in cooperation between police, customs and judicial authorities; enhancement of the role of Europol (the European Police Office); and greater involvement by the European Parliament and the Court of Justice. These developments will build on what has been achieved so far.

Hubs of the drug trade in Europe

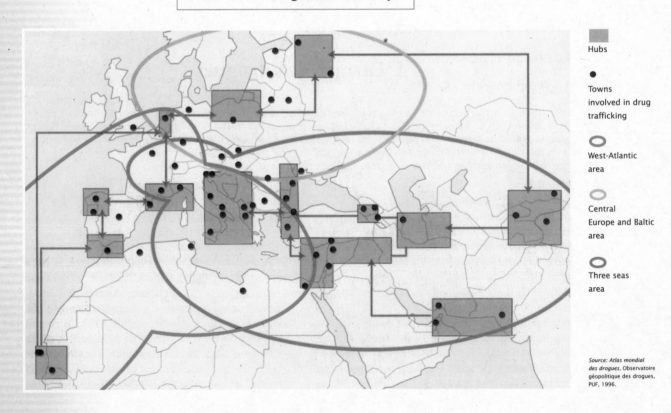

Hubs

● Towns involved in drug trafficking

○ West-Atlantic area

○ Central Europe and Baltic area

○ Three seas area

Source: Atlas mondial des drogues, Observatoire géopolitique des drogues, PUF, 1996.

2.1. Action so far in relation to drug supply

Action against drug supply has international, European and national dimensions. In 1987 the United Nations held a world conference on drug trafficking, where the European Community was represented. This conference prompted the European Parliament into supporting the international fight against drugs with a financial contribution of ECU 5 million. In 1988 the Community signed the **United Nations Convention against Illicit Traffic in Narcotic Drugs and Psychotropic Substances** ('Vienna Convention').

More specifically in the European context, the stimulus for much of the EU's cooperation against drug trafficking was the Single European Act of 1987. The Act established the concept of a single market within the borders of the European Community, which would allow for the free movement of people, services, capital and goods. The EU has taken action to prevent drug traffickers using 'free movement' for their own ends.

This action has taken three main forms:

›   police cooperation against drug trafficking whenever it involves two or more Member States, and customs cooperation;

›   action against money laundering, to prevent traffickers being able first to hide and then to enjoy the profits of their crimes;

›   and action against diversion of precursors (meaning the utilization of otherwise legal chemicals to make illegal drugs).

› Police cooperation: Europol

The Europol Convention lays down Europol's primary objective — to improve the effectiveness and cooperation of the appropriate authorities in the Member States to combat specific forms of organized crime affecting the EU. The Europol Drugs Unit was the first element of Europol to begin its work, in 1994, as a non-operational unit. Europol supports the work of the police and other appropriate authorities in the Member States, ensuring among other things:

›   the exchange and analysis of intelligence on drug trafficking;

›   training for members of police forces and related agencies.

Based in The Hague in the Netherlands, Europol is made up of both liaison officers and its own staff. It acts as a focus for the exchange of information between the police forces of the Member States, but it is not a 'super force', able to pursue criminals from one country to another.

› Action against money laundering

Just as drugs and traffickers can move from country to country, so too can money. In our electronic age, vast amounts of money can and do move around the world in seconds. 'Dirty' money — the profits of crime, including the profits of drug trafficking — can easily be mixed with clean money from legitimate transactions. As this money distances itself from its sources, sometimes going through international financial centres where controls are less than strict, it finally comes out looking indistinguishable from legally obtained money.

This is 'money laundering'. Traffickers and other criminals launder their profits in order to be able to spend it on a luxurious lifestyle — or to invest it in parts of the legitimate economy. This distorts the financial sector and could undermine whole national economies.

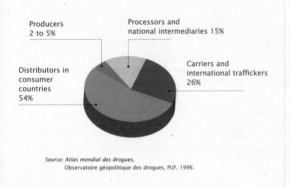

Who gains most from the trade in illicit drugs

Producers
2 to 5%

Processors and
national intermediaries 15%

Distributors in
consumer
countries
54%

Carriers and
international traffickers
26%

Source: Atlas mondial des drogues,
Observatoire géopolitique des drogues, PUF, 1996.

To counter this, the European Community has maintained a keen interest in making sure that financial institutions, such as banks, report suspicious financial transactions. A directive, adopted in 1991, requires Member States to take action to ensure that the financial system is protected against money laundering:

› Financial institutions are required to ask for details of customers' identity, to keep transaction records, and to provide information to the authorities if there are any grounds for suspicion.

› And bank secrecy must be lifted whenever money laundering is suspected. This means that banks have to give the authorities access to information about the account of any customer who is suspected of involvement in laundering money from drug trafficking.

The European Parliament takes a very close interest in efforts to prevent money laundering. It has discussed how best to bring non-financial professions under the provisions of the money laundering directive. It is also pushing for the widening of the law to include new offences. Apart from these Community aspects, the EU Member States, with the support of the Europol Drugs Unit, are working on several projects for the improvement of cooperation between law enforcement services.

On a broader international front, the European Commission participates in the Financial Action Task Force (FATF). Set up in 1989 and run from the offices of the Organization for Economic Cooperation and Development (OECD), the task force is an international body whose purpose is to develop and promote policies to prevent money laundering. The FATF has drawn up 40 recommendations, setting out the basic framework for anti-laundering efforts. These recommendations cover the criminal justice system and law enforcement, regulation of the financial system, and international cooperation.

› **Action against precursor chemicals**

Precursors are chemicals, sometimes quite common ones, that may be used perfectly legally in chemical industries throughout the world. However, there is a considerable problem of such chemicals being diverted to improper use — such as the synthesis of drugs (amphetamines, 'ecstasy', etc.), or the refining of drugs from plant matter (for example, from coca plant to cocaine, or from opium to heroin).

As part of its responsibility over commercial policy, the European Community has for some time been able to use its regulatory powers to control the trade in and manufacture of precursor chemicals. The Community had turned its full attention to precursors from the time it became involved in negotiations leading up to the signing of the 'Vienna Convention' on drug trafficking. This interest took practical effect, in 1990, through European Community regulations and directives, controlling and monitoring the placing on the market of substances used in the illicit manufacturing of narcotic drugs and psychotropic substances as well as the diversion of precursors in international trade.

Several systems support this policy:

› in 1994, Prexco was set up, a Union-wide computer network which allows Member States to check precursor exports from the Community to other countries, because these chemicals might be used to produce illegal drugs;

› there is also a network which allows public health authorities, as well as the police, to exchange information on precursors with customs — the SCENT e-mail network. A further electronic network gives access to sensitive customs databases — the customs information system.

The Commission has tightened up the rules on the level of details required from the manufacturers and exporters when applying for precursor export licences. It has also begun to involve the industry in its deliberations, thus extending the cooperative ethos outside the narrow bounds of the criminal justice system. And the EU has extended anti-precursor action beyond its own borders (see international section).

2.2. Recent developments in law enforcement

During 1996, Member States took steps to improve practical aspects of cooperation against drug trafficking and drug tourism, and to make penalties more similar in the Member States.

> **Cooperation between national authorities**

Agreement has been reached to examine ways in which the administrative procedures of police services and customs could be made more compatible, so that cooperation against drug trafficking can be made swifter and more effective. At present, the diversity of forms of organization and working methods can impede cooperation, and the Member States have committed themselves to reducing these obstacles.

Cooperation with the private sector is also being stepped up, through memoranda of understanding between customs and businesses. This is not only a European trend, but also an international one — as a letter written to the London-based *Financial Times* newspaper by the Secretary-General of the Paris-based International Chamber of Commerce (ICC) makes clear:

'The ICC's role would be to encourage its thousands of member companies all over the world to implement anti-smuggling programmes in partnership with customs. The need becomes more urgent in view of the growing complexity of international trade. The lengthening chain from raw materials to finished products and the growing numbers of components of different origins in goods traded across borders are among factors helping smugglers to pass contraband uninhibited.'

Closer business-customs partnerships are intended to reduce the opportunities for major trafficking under cover of licit trade. During 1996 the EU also took action on drug tourism, illicit cultivation of drugs, illicit production and national drug laws and penalties.

> **'Approximation' of national laws and penalties**

At the end of 1996, Member States agreed to:

> endeavour to approximate their laws to make them mutually compatible to the extent necessary to prevent and combat illegal drug trafficking in the Union;

> make it an offence publicly and intentionally to incite or induce others, by any means, to commit offences of illicit use or production of narcotic drugs;

> ensure that penalties for trafficking are amongst the most severe penalties available for crimes of comparable gravity;

> and fill legal vacuums regarding synthetic drugs.

What this means is that Member States' legislation will become more similar.

› The question of further harmonization

Besides these recent moves to make Member States' drug laws more compatible, the Council of Ministers has also considered the desirability of harmonizing such laws in all the Member States. The EU has committed itself to examine the extent to which harmonization of Member States' laws could contribute to reducing the consumption and supply of drugs in the EU.

The reader is asked to note that the commitment made in this respect is to examine the extent to which harmonization of laws could contribute to a reduction in drug consumption and supply.

Of course, some legislation is already partially harmonized, insofar as it is a Community responsibility: the reader is referred to obligations of Member States in relation to money laundering and precursors (above). But there is more variability in other areas of law, which traditionally fall within the criminal laws of Member States, or within their administrative measures. In some cases, there is also some regional or local determination of lower levels of drug control (for example, controls on drug use or possession). The question may be, how much do such laws actually vary?

› National laws against trafficking and possession of drugs

Members States' drug laws are, on the one hand, rooted in a world order framed by the provisions of three United Nations international conventions. Nearly all Member States are party to these conventions — the Single Convention on Narcotic Drugs (1961), the Convention on Psychotropic Drugs (1971) and the previously mentioned Convention against Illicit Traffic in Narcotic Drugs and Psychotropic Substances (1988).

On the other hand, Member States' drug laws are rooted in their own legal systems. Some EU Member States make distinctions between different drug types, according to the perceived health and social risks to individuals and to society at large. Distinctions may also be made between different types of possession — whether for the purpose of personal use (which in itself is not always criminalized), or for trafficking. Other Member States, however, do not make these distinctions.

The variations in Member States' legislation was one of the topics explored at a **Conference on Drug Policy in Europe**, convened by the EU at the end of 1995. Expert legal research prepared for that conference showed that:

›   first, of course, as already mentioned above, legislation on money laundering and precursors is already broadly harmonized, since these areas are covered by Community legislation;

›   drug trafficking itself — or possession of drugs with the intention of supplying them to other people — is heavily penalized in all Member States (especially when it involves large quantities, and/or importation, and/or minors, depending on the laws of particular Member States). In this dimension, therefore, there is already a degree of similarity between the laws and legal practices of Member States;

›   as far as use of drugs is concerned (or possession not for supply), the laws of Member States appear quite diverse. But the implementation of those laws seems to result in similar practices. Quite often, drug users may be given a warning, a fine or other relatively minor sanctions (short of imprisonment);

›   and as far as dependent persons are concerned, even when prosecution does occur, there are generally provisions for treatment, as an alternative to imprisonment. This may be called diversion from the criminal justice system.

Thus one possibility may be that, at each of these levels of control, the degree of approximation is already quite developed.

Meanwhile, it has been appreciated by the EU that the best laws are those which are enforced — and that differences between the procedures of the many enforcement and judicial agencies within Member States can pose impediments to full cooperation in practice. So, from 1996 onwards, attention also turned to practical improvements in European cooperation against trafficking.

These two elements — the continuing debate over further formal convergence of laws, and on ways of improving practical aspects of cooperation — sum up the EU's search for more effective anti-trafficking action.

› **The draft Treaty of Amsterdam**

Finally, on police and judicial cooperation, the new draft Treaty of Amsterdam sets out the arrangements within which, from 1999 onwards, the EU will take action to provide citizens with a high level of safety. This is to be done by preventing and combating crime, organized or otherwise, including drug trafficking.

The three means envisaged for tackling drug trafficking are: closer cooperation between police forces, customs authorities and other competent authorities in the Member States, both directly and through Europol; closer cooperation between judicial and other authorities of the Member States; and the possibility of further approximation of the criminal laws of the Member States.

It is too early to say in detail what this might mean for drugs, but two comments are possible. Firstly, the draft Treaty's reference to crime 'organized or otherwise' suggests that it is not only top-level criminal organizations that will be targeted. Member States are conscious that citizens are concerned about public nuisance aspects — such as local drug dealing in public places, or drug tourism — which have an impact on everyday life.

A second observation could be that much of the cooperation envisaged for the future seems to be rather practical: overcoming geographical and other obstacles to closer cooperation between the many public administrations and agencies which are involved in the fight against crime. This, too, holds promise for the fight against drug supply and related problems of concern to the citizen.

3

International cooperation against drug production, supply and use outside the EU

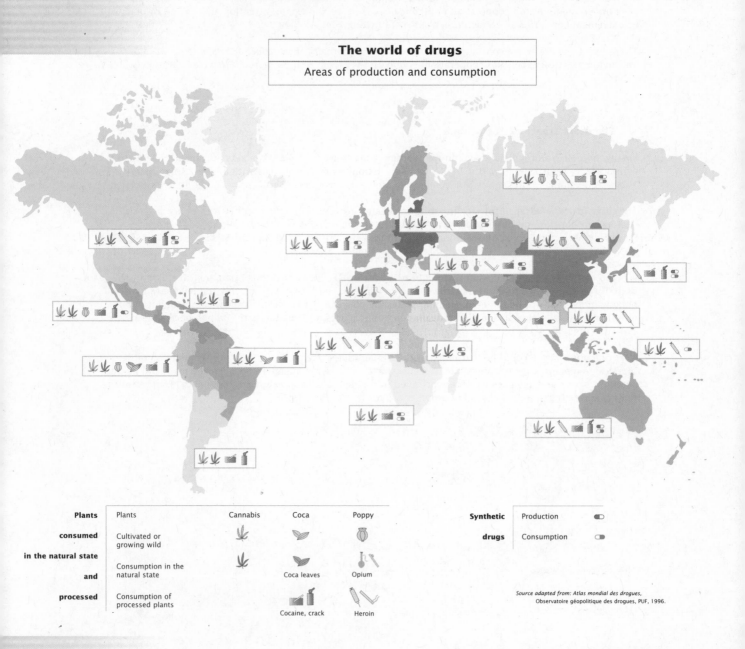

The world of drugs

Areas of production and consumption

Plants	Plants	Cannabis	Coca	Poppy		Synthetic	Production	
consumed	Cultivated or growing wild					drugs	Consumption	
in the natural state								
and	Consumption in the natural state		Coca leaves	Opium				
processed	Consumption of processed plants		Cocaine, crack	Heroin				

Source adapted from: Atlas mondial des drogues,
Observatoire géopolitique des drogues, PUF, 1996.

Drug problems are not only local, national and pan-European in their scope, but also international. The EU, therefore, takes international action with a combination of economic and trade measures, political action and cooperation, assistance through development programmes, control measures and other practical means.

'Close to home', the EU acts in two geographical arenas:

›   in **Central and East European countries**,

›   and to the immediate south and east of the **Mediterranean**.

These activities go hand in hand with action in three other zones of the world, where drugs also pose problems:

> **South-East and Far East Asia** (traditionally, zones of cultivation of the opium poppy, from which opium and heroin may be made), joined more recently by Central Asia;

> some **Latin American countries** (sources of cocaine, cannabis and other drugs, and their transit) and the Caribbean (cannabis, and also transit from Latin America);

> and the **African continent** (where some countries find themselves being a conduit for transit of drugs from other regions, and where there is also illicit cultivation and production).

In each of these spheres, the EU acts to support the development of global and national policies and strategies against drugs. The practical ways in which the EU cooperates with such countries are:

> assistance with the reduction of cultivation of plant crops such as the opium poppy and the coca bush. This assistance can take the form of support for farmers switching from illegal plant crops to legal crops, and infrastructural development, such as roads to get legal crops to the market;

> assistance is sometimes underpinned by favourable terms of trade for legal agricultural crops (fruit, vegetables, flowers) and other products from the region. This is the case for Bolivia, Columbia, Ecuador, Peru, Costa Rica, Guatemala, Honduras, Nicaragua, Panama and El Salvador;

> assistance with the important task of developing countries' legislative frameworks, and the strengthening of the infrastructure and capabilities of their legal systems. Also, assistance with actions against money laundering, against diversion of precursor chemicals, and against drug trafficking itself. Increasingly there is day-to-day cooperation between national enforcement agencies, evaluating intelligence and giving mutual assistance against international drug traffickers;

> as developing countries increasingly suffer from an 'overspill' of illicit plant drugs and synthetic drugs, EU assistance also turns to the prevention of drug use, rehabilitation of drug users and reduction of drug-related public health problems such as HIV/AIDS.

This global cooperation between the EU and developing countries is linked to anti-drug actions by other major developed countries and by international organizations, including the Council of Europe, the World Health Organization and other United Nations agencies. The framework set by the UN underpins many of the international actions of the EU.

3.1. Action so far on international aspects

› **Central and East European countries**

In the broadest context, many Central and East European countries (CEECs) have become linked to the EU through 'Europe Agreements' (Association Agreements). These agreements assist countries which may be candidates for future membership of the EU — or which may desire a close association with it — to bring their economic, political and legislative frameworks and ways of working closer to the standards of Member States of the EU. In short, these CEECs are committing themselves to the *acquis communautaire* (body of established law) of the EU. So, in general terms, what has been outlined earlier in this booklet regarding EU action in relation to drug use and drug supply also applies to the CEECs, as far as their future development is concerned.

However, it is one thing to sign an international agreement, and another thing to be able to implement it fully. This is where the EU's PHARE programme comes in. PHARE aims to help the CEECs, in practical ways, to develop their own (domestic) legislative frameworks and capability to underpin democracy and the rule of law. This broad programme has been extended specifically in relation to drug problems: reduction of drug use, reduction of drug supply, and the networking of information on drugs.

› For example, on demand reduction, pilot projects have been active for some time. Identification of alternative ways of reducing demand in the CEECs (treatment as well as education) led, in 1996, to the appointment of PHARE national drug demand reduction coordinators in each participating country. These coordinators have been able to define their roles and draw up work plans for future activities. By early 1997, six PHARE countries began developing demand reduction strategies with the EU's help.

› On supply reduction, in November 1996, the three Baltic States signed the Riga Declaration on the fight against money laundering. On control of precursor substances (legal chemicals used to manufacture illegal drugs), equipment and training have been provided for the CEECs. These practical steps help translate the new legal commitments of the CEECs into practical cooperation with the authorities in the EU, and into action within the CEECs.

› On the exchange of information, the Union is promoting the development of an electronic information network, so that drug data can be shared between countries in Eastern Europe, and also between them and EU Member States.

These programmes do not aim at directly delivering or supporting anti-drug activities in the CEECs — that would be a mammoth task, and, anyway, is the responsibility of the countries concerned. But the PHARE projects do aim to empower the CEECs to build up their own capability to act, both in relation to the passing of appropriate laws, the implementation of those laws, as well as the development of capabilities on the ground.

› **The new independent States**

Similarly, the TACIS programme channels technical assistance to the former Soviet Union and to Mongolia. The EU has agreed to use this programme to finance action against organized crime and anti-drug activities.

› **Euro-Med partnership and anti-drug action**

The EU's trading relations and security interests to the south also provide a framework for cooperation against drug problems. At the end of 1995, seeds were sown for a Euro-Mediterranean partnership at a conference in Barcelona. The nations reaching agreement with the EU were Turkey, Cyprus, Malta, Egypt, Morocco, Syria, Algeria, Tunisia, Israel, Jordan, Lebanon and the Palestinian-controlled West Bank and Gaza Strip. The aim of the conference was to draw up a formal agreement to 'ensure that the Mediterranean becomes, more so than at present, an area of exchange and dialogue guaranteeing peace, stability and the well-being of those who live around it'.

Action against drug trafficking was singled out as one of the main social and human aspects which the partnership will address. As a result, there has been increased exchange of information and expertise, cooperation between law enforcement agencies, and destruction of drug crops. These activities have been underpinned by the agreement in 1996 of a MEDA programme of financial and technical support for the Euro-Mediterranean partnership, initially to run until 1999.

› The broader canvass of global action

For several decades — for years before the CEECs or the Euro-Med became priority issues — drug-related problems in the Far East and South-East Asia were of serious concern, mostly in relation to heroin. From the 1980s onwards, Latin America and the Caribbean became at least as much a focus for concern, mainly because of cocaine trafficking. During the 1990s, world heroin production and consumption appear to have increased, cocaine has become more widespread, and the trafficking routes have diversified to include the African continent.

The many involvements of the EU in international cooperation against drug production, transit, use and related problems are too numerous to mention here. But it is possible to give the flavour of the activities supported.

The most long-standing context for cooperation against drugs is the North-South programme. This programme is steered by a philosophy of aid, development and co-responsibility: the EU and the country to which funds are being granted work together to ensure that the particular project reaches fruition. For example:

› in Costa Rica, a social rehabilitation project for street children was part-funded by the EU. In Thailand, methadone treatment for drug addicts as well as a programme of economic alternatives to drug cultivation were also funded by the EU. In Ecuador supply reduction was the priority. In Afghanistan, a harm-reduction project for drug users was the key to broader community development;

› similar strategies are in the developmental stage in Africa. In southern Africa, a sub-regional action plan is being drawn up, following a conference hosted by the EU and the South African Development Community. In west Africa, a four-year EU drug control programme has been approved, with the objective of helping the 16 west African countries develop their own national drug strategies.

› Cooperation with regional groups and international organizations and bilateral agreements

The EU strategy is underpinned by agreements with other developed countries such as the United States, Canada and Japan. For example:

› in the first Asia-Europe meeting, in 1996, it was agreed that Japan and China would initiate cooperation with European customs experts. A Euro-Asian working group on enforcement has been set up, including representatives from Japan, China, South Korea and seven countries from the Association of South-East Asian Nations (ASEAN);

› the EU and the United States are working closely to counter trafficking in the Caribbean, buttressing drug enforcement agencies, developing scientific laboratories, improving maritime cooperation (to track and interdict sea-borne drug trafficking) and supporting treatment and cooperation;

› under a 'transatlantic agreement' the EU and the United States focus on improvement of cooperation in relation to the prevention of diversion of precursor chemicals. This allows the EU and the United States to pool sensitive information and to act together to stop shipments to sensitive regions of the world. Cooperation with precursors is also in train with the regional trade blocks ASEAN and Mercosur.

Informal contacts are also maintained through the 'Dublin Group', formed in 1990. Its members are the EU Member States, the European Commission, the United States, Canada, Australia, Norway and Japan. The group hosts working groups on issues relevant to particular regions.

The EU also plays its role in several international organizations working in the field of drugs, most notably the Pompidou Group of the Council of Europe, and the United Nations international drug control programme.

› The Pompidou Group — The Cooperation Group to Combat Drug Abuse and Illicit Trafficking in Drugs — is a constituent part of the Council of Europe. The group, whose members include EU Member States, the European Commission and also many other European and bordering countries, assists countries to develop appropriate drug policies. The EU and the Pompidou Group coordinate their activities.

› The United Nations international drug control programme (UNDCP) provides the broadest context for international cooperation on global drug problems. The European Commission is a member of the UNDCP's informal 'Major Donors' group of 16 and helps to review UNDCP workplans.

In these ways, the EU plays its part in coordinating international action against drugs.

3.2. Recent developments in the international sphere

EU policy on drugs is being linked to issues of regional security, the rule of law, democratization and human rights — as well as continuing to be linked to issues of regional and national economic development, and agreements on trade. For example:

› during 1996, meetings between the EU and the CEECs ('associates' of the Union and in some cases poised to join), focused strongly on drug trafficking and on the scope for improvements in countermeasures. Discussions have examined the present legal situations in these countries — as far as formal existence of laws and actual implementation are concerned — and have looked at trafficking problems. In particular, the so-called Balkan Route, and its fragmentation and re-routing due to regional wars and instability, has been a focus of concern. There will be further regional meetings at expert level on this, on synthetic drugs and on enforcement methods and cooperation;

› in Central Asia, experts working on behalf of the EU have identified problems which include, principally, the transit of drugs, but also drug-related criminality. Here the needs are for development of a legal system capable of acting against trafficking and money laundering, improvement of police cooperation and control at the frontiers;

› the Caribbean and Latin America continue to be important focuses for anti-drug action. EU support has included the buttressing of institutional capabilities to aid prevention, supply reduction, the application of the law, the fight against trafficking and money laundering, and regional cooperation.

It is fair to say that the EU's actions on drugs in the international sphere, far from being peripheral to its wider economic and political policies, is very much integrated within them. This broad and coordinated quality of external anti-drug action reflects the trend within the EU. There, too, responses to drug users have moved from being a somewhat specialized health issue to being a central concern of public health within the EU, and anti-trafficking action has moved to the forefront of the fight against crime (as described in the preceding chapters).

This involvement of so many aspects of external and internal EU policies in the fight against drugs makes it important that politicians, specialists and citizens alike have access to good information on these complex and inter-linked issues, to which we now turn.

4

Sharing of drug information

European policy-makers need good quality information, if drug policies are to be soundly based. The citizen also needs good quality information, in order to understand the issues at stake in drug policy, to be able to formulate an informed opinion and, if she or he wishes, to participate in the democratic debate on the broad directions of drug policy.

If these decisions and debates are to be soundly based, it is essential for the information to be of a high quality. During the 1980s, as drugs increasingly became a concern throughout the EU, it was realized that, in order to get a coherent picture of drug problems, it would be necessary to set up a centre to collate drug information originating from a very wide variety of sources.

4.1. Action taken to improve drug information: the European Monitoring Centre for Drugs and Drug Addiction (EMCDDA)

› **Need for comparability of information at European level**

There are a great number of organizations and agencies involved in responding to drug problems, at all levels of the EU, who have to collect some drug information:

› the Member States, their ministries, departments, regions, municipalities and other authorities collect a mass of information on drug-related matters;

› throughout Europe, non-governmental agencies involved in the fight against drugs also collect and use information in a wide variety of ways;

› the European Commission keeps information on issues within its area of concerns and on the activities the European Community itself carries out or supports;

› this information spans all areas of policy and action: on drug use and responses to it, and on drug supply and countermeasures, within the EU and in the international sphere.

Not only are there many agencies keeping drug information (literally thousands, considering all those involved at local, regional, national and international levels); but the information itself varies enormously. This variety reflects the different requirements of agencies, the topics they find most relevant, and their technical capabilities. The form in which information is collected and kept also varies with organizational differences of scale, as well as national, regional and local traditions. On top of that, of course, there is linguistic diversity. The general outcome is that drug information across the EU is not easily comparable.

› Unless actively tackled, this non-comparability of drug information from different sources and Member States would pose grave problems for cooperation and policy-making on drugs.

› In order for EU Member States and international partners to learn from each other and to cooperate against drug problems, some common systems for handling information have to be evolved.

This highlights the importance of the work of the EMCDDA.

```
┌─────────────────────────────────────────────────────────────┐
│            Information-gathering role of the EMCDDA:          │
│                        priority areas                        │
└─────────────────────────────────────────────────────────────┘
```

A. The work of the centre shall be carried out with due regard to the respective powers of the Community and its Member States in the areas of drugs, as those powers are defined by the Treaty.

The information gathered by the centre shall relate to the following priority areas:

1. demand and reduction of the demand for drugs;

2. national and Community strategies and policies (with special emphasis on international, bilateral and Community policies, action plans, legislation, activities and agreements);

3. international cooperation and geopolitics of supply (with special emphasis on cooperation programmes and information on producer and transit countries);

4. control of trade in narcotics, psychotropic substances and precursors, as provided for in the relevant present or future international conventions and Community acts;

5. implications for producer, consumer and transit countries, within areas covered by the Treaty, including money laundering, as laid down by the relevant present or future Community acts.

B. The Commission shall make available to the centre, for dissemination, the information and statistical data which it possesses pursuant to its powers.

C. During the first three-year period, special attention will be given to demand and demand reduction.

Source: Council Regulation (EEC) No 302/93 of 8 February 1993 on the establishment of a European Monitoring Centre for Drugs and Drug Addiction, Annex.

› Framework for establishment of the EMCDDA

In 1993, following feasibility studies over three years, the European Monitoring Centre for Drugs and Drug Addiction was set up in Lisbon.

Its objective is to provide the European Community and the Member States with an overall view of the drug situation in five 'priority areas': these are reproduced in a box on the page opposite.

Within these areas, the tasks of the centre are:

› to collect and analyse information from the Member States and European Community sources, using surveys, studies, meetings, documentation systems, and other means of exchanging information;

› to improve the comparability of information on drugs, by establishing 'indicators' that can be recommended for adoption and to facilitate databases of information;

› to disseminate information by making it available to the Community, Member States, other States and international organizations, especially through publishing an annual report;

› to cooperate with European and international bodies and organizations and with non-EU countries, to incorporate EU drug information into wider international drug monitoring and policy systems.

Typically, the EMCDDA fulfils its tasks by making calls for tender, or by convening working groups, comprising experts from all the Member States — with the objective of clarifying the basis of existing information-collection methods and, where possible, identifying specific opportunities for the adoption of common methods for collecting information.

To assist the centre in its tasks, a European information network on drugs and drug addiction (Reitox) has also been set up.

› Focal points for the EMCDDA: the Reitox network

Reitox is a network which links up the EMCDDA with so-called 'focal points' in the Member States (and increasingly in other countries) and also with the European Commission.

Focal points are concerned with a two-way transfer of information:

› 'upward' flow of information: from within the Member States (or, in the case of the European Commission, from its various directorates concerned with drugs), to the EMCDDA where it can be collated, analysed and disseminated;

› 'downward' flow of information: from the European level, through the EMCDDA and its focal points, to governments and non-governmental organizations in the Member States.

A list of focal points and ways of contacting them is given in Annex C to this booklet. Some of these focal points, or their associated documentation and information agencies, may also provide more detailed national information for citizens, experts and policy-makers, as well as provide the specific information requirements for the EMCDDA. The Reitox network communicates by e-mail as well as by more traditional means such as telephone and fax. Both the EMCDDA and most of the focal points publish information not only in printed form, but also in electronic form, through the World Wide Web (WWW). Some WWW coordinates are given in Annex C to this booklet. For example, for those with access to the Internet and a WWW browser, the centre can be found at http://www.emcdda.org.

Because some drug policy in Europe is based on EU legislation, commitments and activities, much of the information on these aspects of drug policy originates in the European institutions themselves. The 'drug coordination unit' in the Secretariat-General of the European Commission (Unit SG/C.5) has a role as 'EC focal point' for coordinating drug-related information within the Commission, and sends such information to the EMCDDA. The WWW pages of this unit are being developed. It monitors the implementation of the European plan to combat drugs, the structure of which is included in this booklet. For contact details, see Annex B.

› Outputs of the EMCDDA: annual report, newsletter, monographs...

The most important output of the centre is its annual report on the state of the drug problem in the European Union. Some of the illustrations and tables of data used in this booklet are taken from that report. From 1997 onwards this is to be published in two parts: a first part forming an overview for the general reader, and a second and more detailed part for those with a more specialist interest. The report covers:

› extent of drug use in the general population, patterns of drug use in particular social groups, drug users' contacts with the health, welfare and criminal justice sectors, and patterns of drug supply;

› information on the various ways in which agencies in the Member States are attempting to reduce drug use, drug trafficking and associated problems, and action taken at EU level;

› information sources and documentation centres at national and international levels, and exchanges of information between them.

The EMCDDA newsletter reports on specific tasks and collaborative projects carried out, gives overviews of the work of specific focal points, and reviews other relevant publications and new developments.

4.2. Recent developments: comparable and rapid information

› Work done and work to come

During 1996 and 1997, EMCDDA projects included work on the following:

› ways of improving the quality and comparability of measures of drug use and related problems (including illnesses and deaths);

› a study on drug-related urban crime and public nuisance, aiming to find a way to exchange experiences between city authorities across the EU;

› a WWW-based database of information on programmes and activities aimed at drug users, which is accessible from anywhere for those having access to the WWW;

› evaluation of the state of knowledge on prevention methods and approaches (what works, and how to do such evaluations);

› pilot work on electronic access to Member States' drug-related legislation (whilst the European Commission enabled electronic access to EU legislation);

› ways of improving collaboration between documentation centres in all the Member States — which collate expert papers and other publications in their national languages, in all the disciplines that are relevant to drugs.

Such documentation potentially covers everything from history and international relations, pharmacology, public health measures and social integration, and drug supply issues. A common framework for categorizing information of primary concern to the EMCDDA is being defined, and a feasibility project on technical and electronic cooperation between libraries is in hand. The EMCDDA has its own documentation centre in Lisbon.

The EMCDDA cooperates with Eurostat, the Statistical Office of the European Communities, which has started to collect statistics related to drug use (collection of information through the insertion of questions on drugs in broader national health surveys, and collection of information on drug-related deaths).

› The rapid information system

As drug phenomena evolve, so too do the information methods of the EU. In June 1997, action was agreed on exchange of information, risk assessment and the control of new synthetic drugs. The main elements are:

› the setting-up of a 'rapid information system' on new synthetic drugs (sometimes called 'dance drugs') and on trends in their supply, availability, use and risks;

› the synthesis of relevant information by the EMCDDA and Europol, both of which will receive information from the Member States;

› the establishment of a risk-assessment procedure, which will be carried out by the EMCDDA together with partners. The risks to be assessed are health risks, social risks and trafficking risks;

› a procedure for agreeing whether to bring new synthetic drugs under greater control, if the risks seem to merit it. That decision will be taken by the Council of Ministers, on the basis of the risk assessment.

New initiatives like this illustrate the way in which specific triggers for closer cooperation between the Member States can overcome national and sectorial barriers, to develop information that is broadly-based, timely and relevant to policy and action.

Finally, in 1997, the Management Board of the EMCDDA agreed that its forward workplan 1999-2000 should include the opening-up of work in its second priority area: national and Community strategies and policies (with special emphasis on international, bilateral and Community policies, action plans, legislation, activities and agreements). This is subject to such work not being detrimental to the work already in hand (as far as the limited resources available to the centre are concerned). It illustrates the development planned for the centre, from those areas which are most 'traditional' in drug information (information on drug users, etc.), through the broader range of information on the drug situation within the EU, towards the international sphere. This span of information reflects the areas in which the European Union is involved in political and practical actions against drugs, as set out in earlier pages.

Overview of funding in 1995

ANNEX A

European Union sources of funding

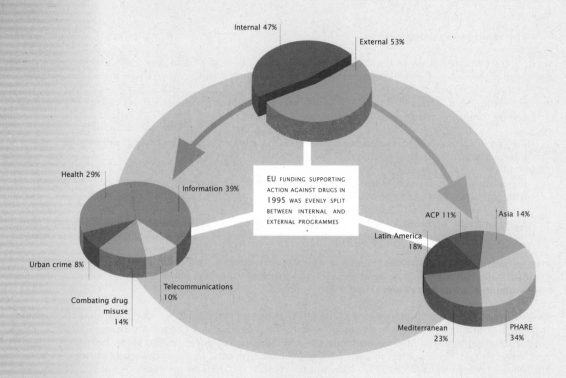

Internal 47%

External 53%

Health 29%

Information 39%

Urban crime 8%

Combating drug
misuse
14%

Telecommunications
10%

EU FUNDING SUPPORTING
ACTION AGAINST DRUGS IN
1995 WAS EVENLY SPLIT
BETWEEN INTERNAL AND
EXTERNAL PROGRAMMES

ACP 11%

Asia 14%

Latin America
18%

Mediterranean
23%

PHARE
34%

Source: Annual report on the state of the drugs problem
in the European Union — 1995, EMCDDA, 1996.

This table mentions some of the EU budget lines which are either entirely devoted to the fight against drugs or allow financing of drug-related projects. The financing criteria vary with the programme concerned, and details may be obtained from the Directorate-General mentioned in the table.

Some examples of current EU funding opportunities

Subject	Objective	Contact point in the Commission	Budget line	Ecus available in 1996
FUNDING INSIDE THE EU				
Health aspects of drug abuse	Promote information exchanges, establishment of networks, campaigns and training of professionals in the prevention field NB: in 1997, it becomes the Community action programme on drug prevention 1996-99	Directorate-General V	B3-4 302	6 500 000 [1]
Measures to combat drug abuse	Implement the various aspects of the EU global action plan on drugs	Secretariat-General/C.5	B3-4 400	2 000 000 [1]
European Monitoring Centre for Drugs and Drug Addiction	Harmonize data collection in the field of drug demand reduction	Secretariat-General/C.5	B3-4 410	5 840 000 [1]
Cooperation in the field of justice and home affairs	Fund common action on cooperation in the field of justice and home affairs Specific programmes	Secretariat-General: Task force for justice and home affairs	B5-8 000	5 500 000 [2]
OISIN:	Enhance cooperation between law enforcement authorities			
Grotius:	Develop training, exchange and work programmes for those in the criminal justice system			
FUNDING OUTSIDE THE EU				
North-South cooperation in the field of drugs and drug addiction	Contribute directly to developing countries in the field of drug demand reduction and supply reduction; contribute to UNDCP	Directorates-General IB and VIII	B7-6 210	10 000 000 [1]
Financial and technical cooperation with Latin American countries	Develop projects related to macro-economic and sectorial problems, including the fight against drugs	Directorate-General IB	B7-3 100	30 000 000 [1]
PHARE multicountry programme for the fight against drugs	Multidisciplinary support to Central and East European countries in the field of drugs	Directorate-General IA	B7-5 000	5 000 000 [1]
PHARE LIEN (Link Inter European NGO's) programme	Support non-governmental organizations from Central and East European countries, working in the social sector in favour of disadvantaged groups of the population	Directorate-General IA	B7-5 000	10 000 000 [2]
European Development Fund (Lomé Convention)	Support measures preventing drug abuse and drug trafficking in ACP countries at regional and interregional level	Directorate-General VIII	B7-1 000	980 000 [1]

[1] Amount specifically devoted to actions in the field of drugs.

[2] Total amount allocated to the programme, which allows financing of drug-related projects.

Who does what on drugs in the EU?
Overview of the Parliament, Council and Commission

	PARLIAMENT	COUNCIL	COMMISSION
	Rue Belliard 97/113 B-1040 Brussels Tel. (32-2) 284 21 11 Fax (32-2) 230 69 33	Rue de la Loi 175 B-1048 Brussels Tel. (32-2) 285 61 11 Fax (32-2) 285 73 81	Rue de la Loi 200 B-1049 Brussels Tel. (32-2) 299 11 .11 Fax (32-2) 295 01 38/39/40
INTERNAL COORDINATION	Committee on Civil Liberties and Internal Affairs	Directorate H Justice and home affairs	Secretariat-General Unit C.5
DEMAND REDUCTION	Committee on Environment, Public Health and Consumer Protection Committee on Social Affairs Committee on Culture, Youth, Education and the Media	Directorate F Economic and social affairs	Directorate-General V Directorate-General XXII
TRADE COOPERATION money laundering, precursors	Committee on Economy, Monetary and Industrial Policy Committee on External Economic Relations	Directorate C Internal market the Custom Union, industrial policy Approximation of laws	Directorates-General I, IA, IB, III, XV, XXI
DEVELOPMENT COOPERATION	Committee on Development and Cooperation Committee on External Economic Relations Committee on Agriculture	Directorate E External economic relations, common foreign and security policy (CFSP)	Directorate-General IA Directorate-General IB Directorate-General VIII
JUSTICE AND HOME AFFAIRS	Committee on Civil Liberties and Internal Affairs	Directorate H Justice and home affairs	Secretariat-General Task Force 2 (Title VI of the Treaty)
COMMON FOREIGN AND SECURITY POLICY	Committee on Foreign Affairs, Security and Defence Policy Committee on External Economic Relations	Directorate E External economic relations, common foreign and security policy (CFSP)	Directorate-General IA Directorate-General IB

Source adapted from: Annual report on the state of the drugs problem
in the European Union — 1995, EMCDDA, 1996

Commission services in action against drugs

Coordination and cross-sectoral issues:
In the Secretariat-General, Unit C.5 provides coordination of all drug-related activities within the Commission. It also provides the Commission with a focal point in the Reitox network (European information network on drugs and drug addiction). This ensures a flow of relevant information between all the Commission services concerned with drugs (see below) and the EMCDDA in Lisbon (described in Section 4 above).

In Directorate-General III (Industry), Unit B.6 (European telematics networks and systems and IDA — exchange programme of data between administrations) manages the IDA telecommunications programme on interchange of data between administrations, including such projects relating to the EMCDDA and the Reitox network (European information network on drugs and drug addiction).

In Eurostat, the Statistical Office of the European Community, Directorate D (Social and regional statistics), which has started activities on statistics related to drug demand, manages the statistical framework programme 1993-97, the statistical framework programme for the years 1998-2000 being in preparation.

Drug actions focusing on drug users and health:
In Directorate-General V (Employment, Industrial Relations and Social Affairs), Unit F.2 (Action programmes targeted on diseases), Unit F.1 (Public health: analyses, coordination, development and assessment of policies and programmes) and Unit F.3 (Promotion of health and monitoring of diseases), deal with prevention aspects.

In Directorate-General XII (Science, Research and Development), Unit E.4 (Medical research) is responsible for medical research within research and development, including drugs (Biomed 2). The ambit of DG XII also covers research into the detection of drugs, which can apply to users or to supply. Directorate G (Targeted socio-economic research) works on the research on social exclusion and social integration within the targeted socio-economic research programme.

Drug actions focusing on drug supply:
In the Secretariat-General, Unit 2 (Police and customs cooperation) of the Title VI TEU Task Force (Cooperation on justice and internal affairs) includes a sector on cooperation in the field of drugs. This deals with drug-related customs and police issues. Unit 3 covers internationally organized crime, which includes money laundering.

In Directorate-General III (Industry), Unit C.4 (Chemicals, plastic and rubber) manages the implementation of Council Directive 92/109/EEC which aims at combating the diversion of chemical precursors.

In Directorate-General XV (Internal Market and Financial Services), Unit C.1 (Banks and financial establishments) focuses on action against money laundering. A report on the implementation of the Council Directive of 10 June 1991 has to be drawn up by the Commission at least every three years.

In Directorate General XXI (Customs and Indirect Taxation), Unit A.2 (Prevention and prosecution of fraud) works on administrative cooperation against the diversion of precursors (external trade aspects).

Drug actions in the international sphere:
In Directorate-General I (External Relations: Commercial Policy and Relations with North America, the Far East, Australia and New Zealand), Unit B.1 (United States) and Unit B.2 (Australia, New Zealand, Canada, NAFTA and APEC) coordinate work relating to bilateral dealings respectively with the United States (transatlantic dialogue, US/EC summits, etc.) and the other countries and regions concerned. Unit F.1 (Japan) and Unit F.2 (China, Korea, Hong Kong, Macao and Taiwan) coordinate work relating to bilateral dealings with the countries concerned.

In Directorate-General IA (External Relations: Europe and the New Independent States, Common Foreign and Security Policy and External Missions), Unit A.3 (Relations with the United Nations) coordinates the Commission's activities relating to action against drugs and the EU's common foreign and security policy. Unit B.6 coordinates PHARE programme assistance to 11 countries covering all aspects of action against drugs. Unit C.1 coordinates TACIS programme assistance for action against drugs. Directorate D, on relations with other European countries (covers EFTA countries, Cyprus, Malta and Turkey, Albania and the countries of former Yugoslavia other than Slovenia), has a role on drugs with these countries.

In Directorate-General IB (External Relations: Southern Mediterranean, Middle East, Latin America, South and South-East Asia and North-South Cooperation), Unit D.2 (North-South relations — Economic relations with international organizations) includes a sector (Sustainable development and anti-drugs coordination) which plays a specific role in coordination of external action against drugs. This covers the southern Mediterranean and Middle East, Latin America and South and South-East Asia.

In Directorate-General VIII (Development), Unit A.2 (Social and Human Development, and Women and Development) is responsible for action against drugs in the African, Caribbean and Pacific (ACP) countries. Western Africa, South Africa and the Caribbean have been identified as the main targets of action in this area.

Contact points in Member States
Reitox focal points

Contact points in Member States

Country	Name	Organization/Address	Phone	Fax	E-mail
Austria	Ms Sabine HAAS	Österreichisches Bundesinstitut für Gesundheitswesen, Stubenring 6, A-1010 Wien	(43-1) 515 61 60	(43-1) 513 84 72	100125.2007@compuserve.com Sabine.Haas@reitox.net
Belgium	Dr Pierre DE PLAEN	Institut Scientifique de la Santé Publique / Wetenschappelijk Instituut Volksgezondheid Louis Pasteur, Rue Juliette Wytsmanstraat 14, B-1050 Brussels	(32-2) 642 50 24 /51 11	(32-2) 642 54 10	Pierre.de.Plaen@reitox.net Françoise.Claeys@reitox.net
Denmark	Ms Vibeke GRAFF	Sundhedsstyrelsen, Amaliegade 13, Postbox 2020, DK-1012 København	(45-33) 9116 01	(45-33) 931 636	vig@sst.dk
Finland	Mr Ari VIRTANEN	Sosiaali-Ja Terveysalan Tutkimus-Ja Kehittämiskeskus, Siltasaarenkatu, 18C (3rd Floor) PO Box 220, FIN-00531 Helsinki	(358-9) 39 67 23 78	(358-9) 39 67 23 24	ariv@stakes.fi Ari.Virtanen@reitox.net
France	Mr Jean-Michel COSTES	Observatoire Français des Drogues et des Toxicomanies, 105 rue Lafayette, F-75110 Paris	(33-1) 53 20 16 16	(33-1) 53 20 16 00	Jean-Michel.Costes@reitox.net
Germany	Mr Roland SIMON	Institut für Therapieforschung, Parzivalstraße 25, D-80804 München	(49-89) 36 08 04 60	(49-89) 36 08 04 69	Roland.Simon@reitox.net
Greece	Dr Anna KOKKEVI	University of Mental Health Research Institute (UMHRI), 74 Vassilisis Sophias Avenue, GR-11528 Athina	(30-1) 722 51 09	(30-1) 723 36 90	akokke@ariadne-t.gr Anna.Kokkevi@reitox.net
Ireland	Ms Mary O'BRIEN	Health Research Board, 73 Lower Baggot Street, Dublin 2, Ireland	(353-1) 676 11 76	(353-1) 661 18 56	mary@hrb.ie mary@reitox.net
Italy	Dr Marisa ZOTTA	Ministero dell' interno, Osservatorio permanente sul fenomeno droga, via Cavour 6, I-0184 Roma	(39-6) 488 26 55/ 46 53 98 27	(39-6) 474 66 11/ 46 53 99 64	Marisa.Zotta@reitox.net
Luxembourg	Mr Alain ORIGER	Ministère de la Santé — Service d'action socio-thérapeutique, 1 rue du Plébiscite, L-2341 Luxembourg	(352) 40 47 40	(352) 40 47 05	Alain.Origer@reitox.net
Norway	Mr Stein BERG	Rusmiddeldirektoratet, Øvre Slottsgate 2b, P.O. Boks 8152 N-Dep-0033 Oslo	(47-22) 24 65 00	(47-22) 24 65 25	stein.berg@rusdir.dep.telemax.no
Portugal	Dr Nuno FELIX DA COSTA	Observatório VIDA, Av Columbano Bordalo Pinheiro 87-2, P-1000 Lisboa	(351-1) 721 02 70	(351-1) 727 38 03	nfc@obvida.pt
Spain	Mr Camilio VAZQUEZ	Delegacion del Gobierno para el Plan Nacional sobre Drogas, C/Fernando el Santo 23, E-28010 Madrid	(34-1) 537 27 25	(34-1) 537 27 08	Delafuente@sgiie.pnd.es
Sweden	Ms Ylva ARNHOFF	Folkhälsoinstitutet, Office Olof Palmes gata 17, S-103 52 Stockholm	(46-8) 56 61 35 00	(46-8) 56 61 35 05	Ylva.Arnhof@reitox.net
Netherlands	Mr Frits KNAACK	Trimbos Instituut, Da Costakade 45, P.O. Box 725, 3500 AS Utrecht, Netherlands	(31-30) 297 11 25/86/00	(31-30) 297 11 28/87/11	Frits.Knaack@reitox.net
United Kingdom	Ms Anna BRADLEY	Institute for the Study of Drug Dependence (ISDD), 32-36 Loman Street, London SE1 0EE United Kingdom	(44-171) 928 12 11	(44-171) 928 17 71	Anna.Bradley@reitox.net Nicholas.Dorn@reitox.net Pascaled@isdd.co.uk
European Commission	Ms Hilde VAN LINDT	European Commission, Unit C-5, Rue de la Loi, 200 (N-9 6/la), B-1049 Brussels	(32-2) 296 40 16	(32-2) 295 32 05	Hilde.van-lindt@sg.cec.be

page 32 ← The European Union *in action* against drugs ← 1997